SALT, SUGAR, AND SPICE

WALTER BUEHR

William Morrow and Company   New York

Published simultaneously in Canada by
George J. McLeod Limited, Toronto.
Printed in the United States of America.
Library of Congress Catalog Card Number 69-15873

2   3   4   5   75   74   73   72   71

BY THE SAME AUTHOR

Automobiles, Past and Present

Bread, The Staff of Life

Cloth from Fiber to Fabric

Harvest of the Sea

The Magic of Paper

The Marvel of Glass

Meat from Ranch to Table

Oil, Today's Black Magic

Plastics, The Man-made Miracle

Rubber, Natural and Synthetic

Timber! *Farming Our Forests*

Underground Riches, *The Story of Mining*

Volcano!

Wonder Worker, *The Story of Electricity*

CONTENTS

●

SEASONING

●

Sugar and spice, plus salt—that all-important mineral—are the elements of the art of seasoning. Although often used in small quantities, seasonings can make surprising changes in the taste of meats and vegetables. When they are skillfully added to foods they can create distinctive flavors that bring pleasure and variety to our meals.

We can only guess how man first discovered the amazing effect that salt had on the flavor of his meat. Perhaps he dropped a haunch of game on a seashore rock heavily encrusted with salt, or he may have washed the dirt from his meat by rinsing it in a salt spring—and found it suddenly tasted better.

7

The other seasonings were probably discovered in similar unplanned ways. Some primitive cook may have wrapped his meat in green leaves to keep the sand and ashes out of it while it was roasting, and then found that the leaves had imparted a delightful new taste to his elk steak. Perhaps this discovery led to a search for other flavorful plants.

SALT

●

Although all animals, including man, have a physical need for salt—a compound of sodium chloride—primitive man needed very little extra salt. Most of the food he ate was the raw flesh of other animals, whose blood contained salt. When man began to cook his food, however, it lost much of its natural salt, and he had to add salt to his diet.

As man began to raise his food instead of hunting and gathering it, he started keeping domestic animals, like cattle and sheep. Because they had vegetarian diets, they had to be supplied with chunks of rock salt or salt cakes to lick.

However, the most important use of salt in

early times before the development of canning or refrigeration was for the preservation of food. Most meat animals had to be slaughtered in the fall, because in those days farmers could not store enough hay or other fodder to keep them alive until the spring grasses grew. All fresh meat needed to be preserved with salt to keep it from decaying.

Herring was the chief food of the lower classes in the Middle Ages in Western Europe. Every year enormous catches were brought in, and they too had to be dried and salted or packed in brine, which required many tons of salt. Dairy products—milk, cream, cheese, and butter—had to be heavily salted to keep them from spoiling. Besides its function in preserving food, a great deal of salt was used by medieval leather workers in curing and working hides. Distillers also used salt in making beer and liquor.

Salt became so valuable that it served as money to pay taxes. At one time Roman sol-

diers were given salt as part of their salary, which is the origin of that word. Salt itself was so heavily taxed that only the wealthy could afford it. In medieval days it was customary to offer an honored guest bread and salt, after which his safety in the home was assured. At a banquet the great saltcellar was placed halfway between the head and foot of

the table. The honored guests were seated between the head of the table and the saltcellar.
Those who were seated below the saltcellar were
of humble rank. This custom was the origin of
the expression "to be seated above the salt" or
"below the salt," at dinner.

In early times salt was obtained from brine
wells. The richly saline water was boiled in

huge iron kettles until it evaporated, leaving a deposit of pure, high-quality salt. In hot climates by the sea, salt was obtained in a slightly different way. Seawater was left standing in shallow basins so that the sun would evaporate some of it. The remaining brine was eight times as rich in salt as the original seawater, and the rest of the water could be boiled away without requiring the use of much firewood.

In cool, cloudy, northern Europe it was not possible to begin the evaporation process by using the heat from the sun. After some experimentation salt makers found a way to raise the salt content of seawater. Workers dug up the turf, called peat, from along the water's edge where it was thoroughly soaked with seawater. It was piled on the beach to dry and then set afire to smolder into ashes. The peat ash, rich in salt, was added to huge kettles of seawater. When heated, the strong brine boiled away, leaving fine white salt that was hung in baskets to dry. The peat salt was of good quality,

and because of the great demand for salt, it was produced in such great quantities that the peat beds finally became exhausted. Other methods of salt production then had to be found.

One way made use of the natural process of evaporation. Wherever shallow ponds or marshes lay slightly below sea level along the coast they were cleared of mud and were connected to the sea by narrow channels. The seawater then flowed in at high tide. When the pond was filled the channel was closed by gates, and the water inside slowly began to evaporate in the sun. As the brine thickened it was directed from one basin to another, constantly growing heavier with salt. At last the salt could be scraped up and packed into wicker baskets to finish drying.

Another source of salt that men began to develop were huge underground deposits of the mineral. These deposits had been formed by saline springs dripping for years and years into large cavities in the earth. The water would evaporate leaving caves filled with solid white salt. Sometimes the brine emerged above-ground and ran down a mountain slope. Over a long period of time a salt mountain would be left glittering in the sunshine. Miners dug out the salt by tunneling into it with picks and shovels.

Some of the world's famous underground salt deposits have been worked for centuries. They exist in North Africa, South America, near the Dead Sea, and in Poland, where the famous Wieliczka salt mines near Krakow have been operated for over a thousand years.

In the early days of this mine's operation, the miners, suspended by ropes, swung high up along the walls, hacking out the chunks of salt and letting them drop into the pockets of canvas aprons they wore. When their pockets were filled, the miners slid down the ropes and emp-tied their loads into donkey carts, which were driven to the surface.

In the eighty miles of the Wieliczka mine

tunnels, generations of slave laborers, trying to amuse themselves while working, carved out a whole village in the underground tunnel. Along a main street stand a town hall, churches, a marketplace, complete with counters loaded with meat, fish, fruits, and vegetables. The street is crowded with merchants and shoppers; on a river, float boats filled with villagers. All of this scene is sculptured out of solid salt.

Most modern-day salt mines are worked with electric machinery and lighted by electricity. Salt beds are often discovered far underground by means of electrical instruments. Years ago a salt bed discovered deep underground would have been too difficult or too expensive to mine, but today salt miners know how to reach treasures buried deep beneath the earth's surface.

One method of mining underground salt is by turning it into artificial brine. A large shaft is driven down hundreds of feet to reach a salt bed. Then a smaller pipe is lowered inside the larger one. Water is forced under high pressure

down the large pipe into the salt bed. There it dissolves some of the salt and forms brine, which is pumped up through the inner pipe. The brine is stored in wells until it can be processed.

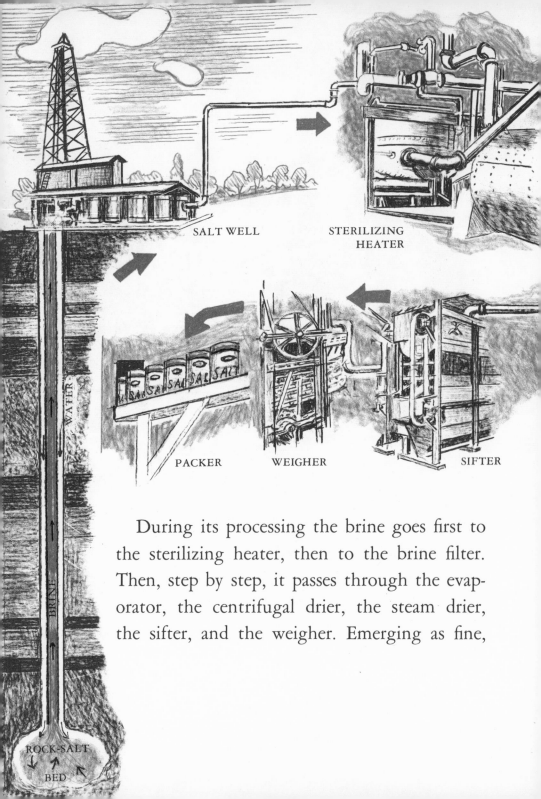

SALT WELL

STERILIZING
HEATER

PACKER WEIGHER SIFTER

During its processing the brine goes first to
the sterilizing heater, then to the brine filter.
Then, step by step, it passes through the evaporator, the centrifugal drier, the steam drier,
the sifter, and the weigher. Emerging as fine,

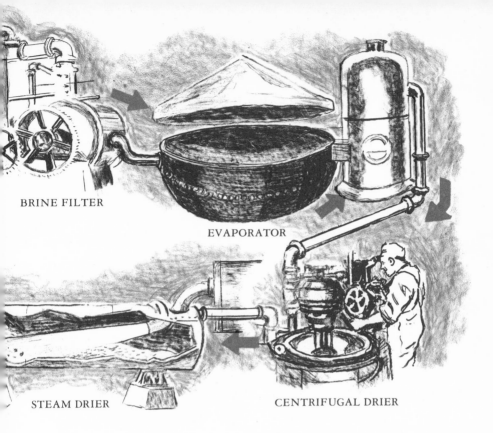

BRINE FILTER

EVAPORATOR

STEAM DRIER

CENTRIFUGAL DRIER

FROM ROCK-SALT BED TO KITCHEN

pure white salt, free of all impurities and moisture, it is packed and sealed in the familiar salt boxes we know, stacked ready for customers on the supermarket shelves.

In this country Syracuse, New York; Lincoln,

Nebraska; Shawneetown, Illinois; Saltsburg, Pennsylvania; and Saltville, Virginia, are among many towns that owe their beginnings to salt making. Detroit, Michigan, lies above great salt deposits from which brine is continually pumped. Today most American salt is prepared by boiling brine inside huge vacuum containers until granules called slurry begin to form. The slurry is drawn off, filtered to remove most of the moisture, and then fully dried in enormous revolving ovens. The use of the vacuum evaporator results in finer, whiter, more evenly sized salt crystals, called granulated salt.

Several localities possess conditions favorable for making salt by solar evaporation. This process is used in California in salt ponds near San Francisco Bay, and along the shore of the Great Salt Lake in Utah. The water of the Great Salt Lake contains from fifteen to twenty-five percent salt, a far higher salt content than that of seawater, which is between two and three percent.

Water from the Great Salt Lake is pumped into square, shallow basins along the shore, early in the summer, usually in May. This water evaporates from the sun's heat, and salt crystals begin to form. The solution is then poured into small "garden" ponds, with floors of salt a foot thick. More salt crystals form and sink to the bottom. The water still remaining is pumped back into the lake. By September three or four inches of new salt have accumulated at the bottom of the garden ponds. It is broken up by tractor plows and stockpiled to await refining and packaging.

SUGAR

•

The desire for sweets is common to all of us. We know that early man was so fond of sweets that he was willing to suffer painfully for them. Cave paintings show naked cave dwellers reaching into a hive in a hollow tree or cave for wild honey, while surrounded by swarms of angry, stinging bees.

For thousands of years sugar has been known in various forms. Sugarcane originated on the Pacific island of New Guinea. For centuries this sweet grass was grown by the natives of tropical islands only because they liked to chew the juice from the canes.

Sugar had been used in the Far East long before it reached Europe. The Arabs brought sugarcane with them to Egypt, Persia, and Spain, along with their knowledge of sugar making. Venetian traders soon began taking to northern Europe and England, along with spices and silks, cargoes of the wonderful new product from the East. Sugar immediately became popular, not only because it tasted so good but because it was believed to have great curative qualities. Apothecaries added sugar to many of their mixtures.

About this time Portuguese and Spanish explorers were ranging far and wide, establishing new colonies. Sugarcane grew well in the climate of most of the colonies. Negroes were brought from Africa to supply the large labor force the crop required. Huge sugar plantations developed in the tropical colonies and prospered for over three hundred years.

The sugar plantation was usually an independent industry of its own. The owner of a plantation grew his crop of cane, crushed the juice out of it in his own mill, and boiled

down the syrup in his own boiler. From some plantations the sacks of raw sugar went by narrow-gauge railroad directly to schooners for shipment to the mainland, where the sugar was refined.

Today most of the old plantations have been bought up by sugar companies. The cane is planted and harvested by large machines, and the raw sugar is finished at the company's own refineries.

A crop of sugarcane proceeds through many steps from planting to refining and packing of the finished product. In late summer the cane field is prepared by being plowed and fertilized.

Sugarcane does not grow from a seed, but from short sections of cane, each containing several buds or nodes. The sections are planted end to end along a furrow, and the first shoots appear above the ground in about a week. The length of time between planting and harvesting varies from eight to thirty months, depending on the growing conditions. By cutting time the stalks reach a height of about fifteen feet.

When the crop is ripe, cane cutters, either mechanical or human, cut the cane in swathes. Some farmers set fire to the crop and burn off the leaves, while the canes, filled to overflowing with sweet juice, remain unharmed by the fire. In any event, the canes are gathered up by cane loaders, which look like tractors with grab forks, or by hand laborers and trucked to the mill where the canes are washed and cut into short sections.

The roots left in the ground sprout again the next two seasons so that three harvests are grown from one planting. The land is then plowed up and allowed to rest or is planted to soy beans, a crop which returns nitrogen to the soil and prepares it for more sugar growing.

At the mill the newly washed cane stalks pass under rows of swiftly moving sharp knives that shred the cane into blanketlike layers of fibers. Three sets of steel rollers squeeze the fibers. The cane juice, a thin yellow liquid about fifteen percent sugar, runs in a torrent from the rollers into tanks. Lime is added to the liquid to carry the nonsugars to the bottom of the tank.

The cane juice is then filtered and boiled several times, until brown sugar crystals begin to form. Then the liquid, which is molasses, is drained off, leaving raw sugar.

Turning raw sugar into refined sugar is a complicated business that took centuries of trial and error and millions of dollars' worth of machinery to perfect. First the raw sugar is dumped into a mingler, where it is mixed with syrup of sugar and water to soften the film of molasses enclosing each crystal.

SEVENTEENTH-CENTURY SUGAR FACTORY

This mixture, called magma, is put in a centrifuge, a large metal basket that spins like a top at very high speed. Water is sprayed in to wash off the molasses coating and fling it out of holes in the centrifuge. The washed sugar goes into a melter where it is dissolved in warm water. The resulting thick syrup is then put through a filter press, which takes out solid impurities. The liquid emerges as clear, washed, sugar liquor.

Still light brown in color, the liquor is pumped into large tanks and filtered again through fine carbon granules. A completely colorless syrup results and is boiled in great vacuum pans in order to crystallize the sugar. In the vacuum pans the air pressure is lowered so that the water in the liquid will boil off at 140 degrees Fahrenheit. At this temperature the sugar will not burn. Each pan produces as much as 50,000 pounds of sugar at a time.

Next the sugar, which still carries a little syrup, goes into a centrifugal to be whirled at high speed and sprayed with water. The remaining syrup is spun off, leaving brilliant white crystals. The sugar then goes into a granulator, a revolving metal drum in which warm air is circulated. The crystals are tossed and tumbled by metal fins and come out pure white, clean, and dry.

The sugar passes next through a series of jiggling screens of varying sizes, which separate it into coarse, standard, or fine granulated sizes.

Some crystals are crushed to make powdered sugar or mixed with clear syrup to be pressed into lumps or cubes.

The final step is packaging the sugar. Containers range from one-half ounce paper packages, just the right size for a cup of coffee or tea, to one-pound boxes for home use or larger containers for bakers, candy makers, ice-cream and soft-drink manufacturers, canners, meat curers, and drug companies.

One other plant, along with sugar cane, serves as a source of more than ninety percent of the world's sugar. This plant is the sugar beet.

Sugar beets have been raised in Europe for many hundreds of years as vegetables, as feed for livestock, and as medicines. Not until 1747, however, did a German chemist, Andreas Marggraf, succeed in producing a spoonful of sugar from beets, but his method was much too costly.

Franz Archard, a pupil of Marggraf, took up

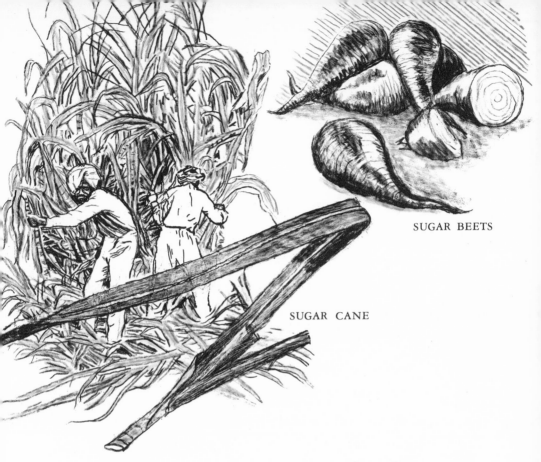

SUGAR BEETS

SUGAR CANE

the search for a cheaper way to produce beet sugar. After thirteen years of constant experiment he succeeded. He built his own beet-sugar mill, but it was not successful because beet sugar could not compete in price with cane sugar.

The Napoleonic Wars, however, established

the importance of beet sugar. Napoleon had closed all European ports to British products and so all sugarcane raised on British West Indian plantations was cut off from the Continent. The people of Europe were soon starved for sugar. Hearing of a sugar mill that produced sugar out of beets, Napoleon visited the plant himself. The emperor was so delighted at the mill's excellent product, which France so urgently needed, that he unpinned his own Legion of Honor medal and pinned it on the breast of the mill owner.

Napoleon ordered thousands of acres to be planted with sugar beets, and within two years forty sugar mills were grinding up beets and turning them into good white sugar. But by 1815 the war was over and Napoleon was in exile. Ships loaded with sugar from the West Indian cane mills were docking at every European port. Sugar-beet growers were still unable to compete with cane sugar and soon all the beet-sugar plants except one were closed.

Still, the beet growers refused to give up. They improved the strains of beet seeds to yield more and sweeter juice, and they redesigned their machinery to work more efficiently. Today beet sugar holds its own in the battle for world markets. Sugarcane supplies two thirds of the world's sugar, and sugar beets furnish most of the rest. The manufacture of beet sugar is similar in many ways to the making of cane sugar. The beets are planted from seed, however, unlike sugarcane. The young beet plants are thinned out and weeded, and they must be irrigated when plentiful rain does not fall during the summer.

By the middle of October the white beets are dug up by a harvester. This machine shakes off most of the dirt, cuts off and drops the tops into the field, and deposits the beets into the tank of the machine. The beets, heavy with juice, weigh from two to five pounds each. At the mill the beets are dropped into a ditch and floated to the washing tank. Next, they go to the slicing machine, which slices them into strips called cossettes. The strips are dumped into tanks of hot water where the sugar soaks out of them. This liquid, called thin juice, is then boiled and evaporated in much the same way as cane juice.

Although sugarcane and beets supply most of the world's sugar, some sugar does come from other sources. One source is the familiar sugar maple tree of our Northeast, which produces a sap that is boiled to make maple sugar. In India and the Eastern tropics the natives

MAPLE SUGAR

make sugar from a palm tree. Each palm produces from forty to eighty pounds of palm
sugar, compared with the three-pound yield of
an average maple tree.

Whatever its origin, sugar is an important
item in our diets, both for its nutritional value
and for the many pleasant-tasting sweets it makes
possible.

SPICES

●

Spices are vegetable products used to season other foods. They may be the seeds, buds, leaves, bark, fruit, or roots of the plant, and they are classified according to their flavor. Pepper, for instance, is a stimulating condiment. Among the aromatic varieties are anise, caraway seeds, cloves, and cinnamon. The sweet herbs—such as rosemary, marjoram, and basil—make up another category.

In medieval days the diet of the average European was extremely limited, consisting mostly of salt meat and fish, bread and pastry, a very few vegetables and fruits, and occasionally honey as sweetening. Most of our familiar vegetables, such as potatoes, tomatoes, and sweet corn, were unknown to medieval cooks. During autumn and winter the fare was dull and tasteless, and would remain so until spring onions, green peas, berries, and peaches ripened, and young lambs and piglets appeared.

In England, where the winter diet was made up of coarse meal and salted meat, most of which had already begun to spoil by springtime, people needed spices desperately to improve the taste of their food. They were eager to have even small quantities of cloves or the other fragrant spices—ginger, cinnamon, and nutmeg. Shipping was so dangerous and expensive in those days that the few condiments that reached the fairs and markets were sold at very high prices. Most spices came initially from faraway places in the East. So many of them originated exclusively in the Moluccas Islands, near New Guinea, that the group came to be known as the Spice Islands.

The Arab traders who brought spices to Europe were eager to keep up the prices of their merchandise. In order to make the spices seem even rarer to their customers, the traders spread tales of the enormous difficulties of obtaining them.

Cinnamon, the Arabs solemnly avowed, grew on trees in the center of a mysterious lake guarded by razor-billed, eaglelike birds. These birds had to be lured to the ground by scattering huge pieces of meat, which they gripped in their claws and clumsily carried to their nests. The weight of the meat broke down the nests and dropped the cinnamon branches to the ground, where the traders gathered them up.

Peppers, the Arabs related, grew on trees swarming with terrible serpents, which could only be destroyed by setting the trees afire and burning up both trees and serpents. Cassia, the story went, grew in shallow lakes guarded by fierce bats from which the gatherers had to be protected by wearing thick cloaks made of ox hides.

During the eleventh century the first of the

great religious crusades began. Thousands of European knights and men-at-arms journeyed either overland or across the Mediterranean to the Holy Land to rescue Jerusalem from the Mohammedan infidels. They soon found that the infidels' way of life, their weapons, armor and clothing, their homes and foods, were far superior to what they had known back in Europe. They grew especially fond of the variety of Eastern spices imported by the Arabs to season their meats and sweet dishes.

When the Crusaders returned home, enterprising Western merchants soon expanded the spice-import business. They established connections with caravans from the Far East and with traders from Cairo and Constantinople. The spices were carried by ship to Venice, to Genoa, and other Mediterranean ports.

After the western and southern coasts of the Mediterranean came under the rule of the Arabs, the spice caravans had to pay higher and higher duties. Finally, the spice trade almost ceased.

Clearly, a new route had to be found along which, the spices of the East could be transported to Europe. Navigator-explorers began searching out ways of reaching India, Ceylon, and the Spice Islands by water.

Much of the interest in exploration originated with the Portuguese. Prince Henry of Portugal established a school of navigation in the windswept halls of his castle on the cliffs of Sagres in southern Portugal. In the summer of 1420 two barques were fitted out and sent southward to explore the mysterious west coast of Africa and discover a passage to the East. The expedition was not successful, and later ones also failed.

Ships under command of Bartolomeo Diaz headed south again in 1488, but a great storm drove them far past the tip of the continent. Diaz wanted to continue the voyage, but the crew insisted on returning home to refit the ship and renew their supplies.

Before another Portuguese expedition got under way, Christopher Columbus decided that the most direct way to reach the Spice Islands was not by sailing southeast around Africa, but by heading straight west. At that time nobody suspected that the two huge continents of North and South America blocked a westbound voyager from reaching the Orient directly. Furthermore, Columbus erred by underestimating the circumference of the earth.

In 1495 King Manuel of Portugal ascended the throne and quickly assembled a new fleet of ships designed by Diaz, under command of Vasco da Gama. The fleet set sail on July 8, 1497, on an incredibly long voyage of 4500 miles, which took them out of sight of land for ninety-six days. They rounded the Cape of Good Hope and on May 21, 1498, almost eleven months after departing Lisbon, the ships at last dropped anchor in the harbor of Calicut, India. The Portuguese immediately began trading with the natives.

As the Portuguese trade expanded in Africa and the East, territories there began to come under Portuguese control. Portugal dominated the spice trade during the sixteenth century. In the next century the Dutch began to wrest from the Portuguese control of the Eastern colonial empire. Presently, the Dutch built their own forts in the Far East, and the Dutch East India Company took over the established trading posts.

For a time the Dutch ruled supreme in the East Indies. They tried to maintain a strict monopoly on the rare spices that grew only in the Spice Islands, which they now controlled. Nobody was permitted to remove seeds from cinnamon, clove, or nutmeg trees. All nutmegs that were to be exported had to be soaked in limewater for three months. This treatment prevented them from germinating and kept the purchasers from growing nutmegs themselves.

Later the British took command of all the spice ports, except Java, and rare spices traveled

the world in British ships. The trade proved as lucrative for this nation as it had for those who had previously dominated it.

The spice trade also affected the development of the United States. For example, Yale University was established partly by the spice trade. Born in Boston in 1649, Elihu Yale was taken to England by his family in 1652, where he received his education. Later he went to India with the British East India Company. He amassed a large fortune there and donated generously to the Collegiate School at Saybrook,

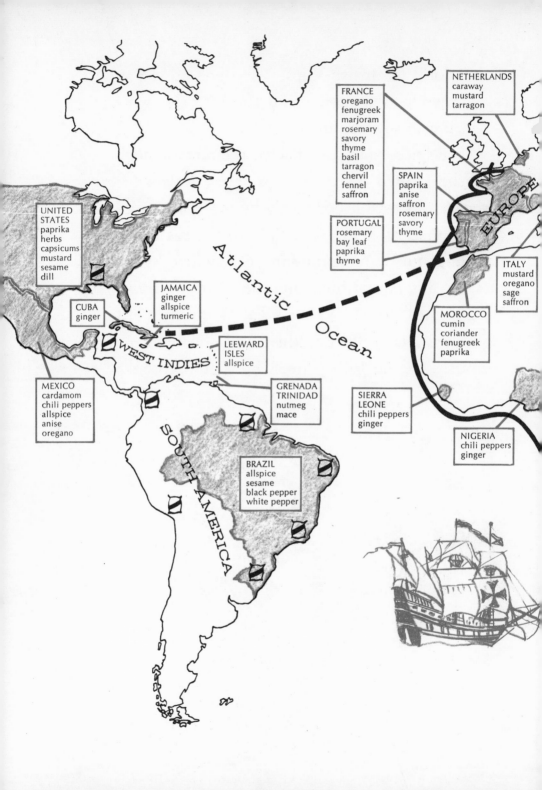

NETHERLANDS
caraway
mustard
tarragon

FRANCE
oregano
fenugreek
marjoram
rosemary
savory
thyme
basil
tarragon
chervil
fennel
saffron

SPAIN
paprika
anise
saffron
rosemary
savory
thyme

EUROPE

UNITED STATES
paprika
herbs
capsicums
mustard
sesame
dill

PORTUGAL
rosemary
bay leaf
paprika
thyme

ITALY
mustard
oregano
sage
saffron

Atlantic Ocean

JAMAICA
ginger
allspice
turmeric

CUBA
ginger

MOROCCO
cumin
coriander
fenugreek
paprika

WEST INDIES

LEEWARD ISLES
allspice

GRENADA TRINIDAD
nutmeg
mace

SIERRA LEONE
chili peppers
ginger

MEXICO
cardamom
chili peppers
allspice
anise
oregano

NIGERIA
chili peppers
ginger

SOUTH AMERICA

BRAZIL
allspice
sesame
black pepper
white pepper

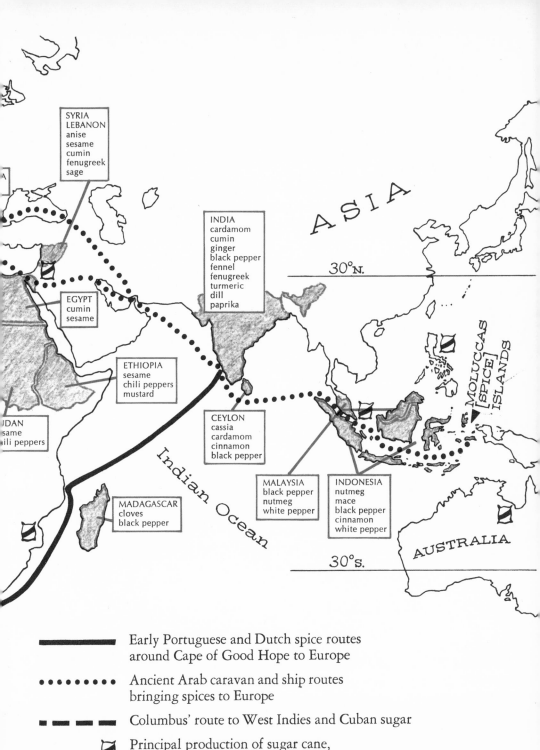

SYRIA
LEBANON
anise
sesame
cumin
fenugreek
sage

INDIA
cardamom
cumin
ginger
black pepper
fennel
fenugreek
turmeric
dill
paprika

ASIA

30°N.

EGYPT
cumin
sesame

ETHIOPIA
sesame
chili peppers
mustard

MOLUCCAS
[SPICE]
ISLANDS

CEYLON
cassia
cardamom
cinnamon
black pepper

JDAN
esame
ili peppers

Indian Ocean

MALAYSIA
black pepper
nutmeg
white pepper

INDONESIA
nutmeg
mace
black pepper
cinnamon
white pepper

MADAGASCAR
cloves
black pepper

AUSTRALIA

30°S.

Early Portuguese and Dutch spice routes
around Cape of Good Hope to Europe

Ancient Arab caravan and ship routes
bringing spices to Europe

Columbus' route to West Indies and Cuban sugar

Principal production of sugar cane,
which grows between lat. 30° N. and 30° S.

Connecticut. After the school was moved to New Haven, its name was changed to Yale College in his honor.

In the eighteenth century America entered the spice trade directly. One April morning in 1788, the brig *Cadet,* under command of Captain Jonathan Carnes, set sail from Salem, Massachusetts for the East. In a port on the coast of Sumatra, Captain Carnes discovered a spice that had never been shipped to the West before. He bought up the product and sailed home with a hold filled with pepper.

The commodity proved valuable, and in 1795 Captain Carnes repeated the voyage. The cargo of pepper carried on this second trip brought a profit of over 700 percent. Soon other American merchantmen began fitting out at every New England yard in order to share in the profitable new trade. In 1818 the import duties on pepper collected in Salem were large enough to pay five percent of the cost of running the United States government for a year.

Originally many spices grew only in remote areas of the world. Those who controlled spice production tried to prevent the plants being grown anywhere else. In some places the penalty of death was invoked against anyone attempting to smuggle seeds of rare spices from their native habitat.

Eventually, though, spices were smuggled out and transplanted in quantity in different parts of the world. India received ginger, black pepper, fennel, fenugreek, and turmeric. Cloves, although they grew best in the Spice Islands, were taken to the East and West Indies and Brazil. Black pepper was successfully transplanted to Zanzibar and Madagascar; chili peppers and ginger were cultivated in Nigeria and Sierra Leone.

The richest and most powerful country in the world has always been the one that controlled the spice trade. In the nineteenth century Britain ruled the waves, and Mincing Lane in London was the center of the spice market.

Today the United States is the leading spice trader, and New York is the chief marketplace. After the spice imports have been inspected by the Pure Food and Drug Administration, they are shipped to processing companies in different parts of the country. There the spices are cleaned, blended, and packaged for the whole-sale and retail trades. Different types of mills are needed for the different forms of raw spices —leaves, barks, and seeds. Also, various buyers want finer or coarser grinds, depending on what use will be made of the product. Spices are packaged in containers ranging from one ounce to 200 pounds. Their users range from house-wives to sausage makers, pickle packers, and many other food processors.

A SPICE LIST

●

Here is a list of spices found in most kitchens today. Some of them have been widely used since medieval times; others have been characteristic of the cooking of one particular country.

ALLSPICE

Allspice is a mildly pungent and aromatic berry of a West Indian myrtle tree. It is the only major spice grown exclusively in the Western hemisphere. The name allspice was given to this seasoning because it combined the fragrance and flavor of cinnamon, cloves, and nutmeg. The allspice tree is a beautiful tropical evergreen, bearing a fruit about the size of a currant. The berries are picked green and dried for a week until they turn a dark reddish brown. Most allspice comes from the island of Jamaica today, but it is also grown in Mexico, Guatemala, Honduras, Brazil, and the Leeward Islands.

ANISE

Anise is an herb native to southwest Asia, northern Africa, and southeastern Europe. The plant also has been introduced to temperate regions in both hemispheres. Anise is a dainty, white-flowered annual, about eighteen inches high, with secondary featherlike leaflets of bright

ALLSPICE

green. The greenish-gray seeds of the plant are used as a flavoring in cakes, pastry, and confectionery.

BASIL

Sweet basil is one of the best liked herbs in today's kitchens. The plant grows to a height of eighteen inches in warm climates. The leaves have a sharp licorice taste when fresh, and a spicy fragrance combining lemon, anise, and resin when dried. In former times one of the main reasons for using spices was to make un-palatable foods taste better, or inexpensive foods

ANISE

BASIL

taste delightful. This ability basil has in full measure.

BAY LEAF

In southern regions the bay tree, one of the laurel family, grows to over thirty feet in height, with beautiful rich, deep green leaves, heavily but pleasantly aromatic. The leaves of the bay tree are laden with an oil used in medicine and cookery.

CARAWAY

Caraway seeds are obtained from a white-flowered perennial herb. The plant originated in Europe,

BAY LEAF

CARAWAY

but it has spread widely and now can be found almost anywhere on the globe. The light brown aromatic seeds are used in cakes, cheese, rye bread, and in preparing some toilet goods.

CARDAMOM

The aromatic seeds of the herb cardamom are used as a condiment and in the preparation of medicines. Originating in the East Indies, the plant was imported into Europe in the thirteenth century. The seeds are contained in a russet-color, fig-shaped fruit. Today cardamom is cultivated in Central America and Mexico and is used in desserts, sausages, and curry powder.

CARDAMOM

CASSIA

The spice cassia comes from the bark of a Chinese tree and is also called Chinese cinnamon. It has a slightly stronger flavor than Ceylon cinnamon. The bark, when peeled off the tree, is a little thicker than parchment and curls up as it dries in the sun. The rolls of bark are tied together with strips of bamboo and shipped in this way. The dried, unripe fruits of the tree, which look like small cloves, are used in making candy. Cassia is now grown in Ceylon, Japan, and South America, as well as in China.

CAYENNE PEPPER

Cayenne pepper, the hot, red pepper, is made by grinding the dried fruit of the cayenne pepper plant. A shrubby perennial plant, it grows two to six feet high and has long red ovate fruit and small flat seeds. Grown originally in Zanzibar, cayenne peppers now grow also in most tropical and subtropical countries.

CASSIA

CAYENNE PEPPER

CHERVIL

The chervil plant is an aromatic Old World herb, similar to parsley but with a milder flavor. It grows to a height of from twelve to twenty-four inches; the stems shoot out numerous branches bearing lacy leaves. These leaves are used in salads, soups, egg dishes, and on fish.

CINNAMON

The familiar spice, cinnamon, is prepared from the bark of the tree of that name. The trunk is covered with a double bark, and after the inner bark has been stripped from the tree and laid on the ground under a hot sun, it curls

CHERVIL

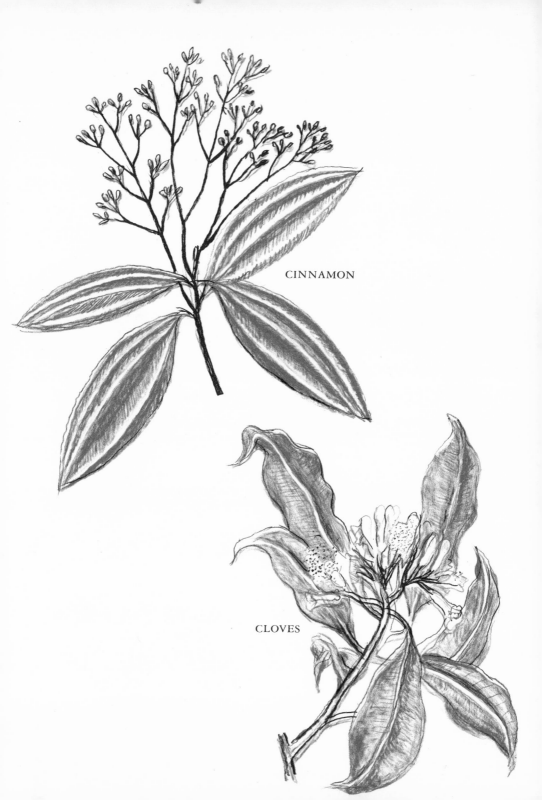

CINNAMON

CLOVES

up like a sheet of wrapping paper. Several sheets of this bark are tied together and shipped as sticks of cinnamon. Later, they may be ground up to make powdered cinnamon. Varying types of cinnamon trees grow in several Asian countries.

CLOVES

Cloves are one of the big four of the spice world, the other most popular spices being pepper, cinnamon, and nutmeg. The clove tree, a tropical evergreen, sometimes grows to a height of forty feet. When buds appear—at first green, then turning bright red—they are picked

before they open into flowers. Then the buds turn brown, which prevents their decaying. Finally, they shrivel up into the brownish black form we are familiar with as a spice. An oil extracted from cloves is used in making medicine and perfume. The clove tree is now successfully cultivated in the West Indies, Zanzibar, and Madagascar, which bears out the old saying that cloves must see the sea in order to prosper.

CORIANDER

Coriander is an Old World herb that originally came from Egypt. The seeds, brownish yellow and the size of peas, have a flavor when dried

CORIANDER

that resembles anise and cumin. They are used in making curry powder and in flavoring meats, pickles, and sauces.

CUMIN

Cumin, a plant whose seeds are used for seasoning, is mentioned several times in the Bible. According to legend, the plant has the power of keeping lovers from straying. Originating in the Nile valley, it has since been introduced into other parts of Africa, and into India and China. Cumin is used today as one of the ingredients of curry powder and as flavoring for chili sauce, cheeses, and pickles.

CUMIN

DILL

Dill is a European herb whose aromatic foliage and seeds are used for flavoring. Dill was originally cultivated in Palestine, and today it grows in areas around the Mediterranean Sea and the Black Sea. During the past 150 years it has also been raised in California. The most familiar use of dill is to make dill pickles.

FENNEL

Fennel is a perennial European herb grown both for foliage and for its seeds, which are used as seasoning. Italians like to eat stalks of fresh fennel as we eat celery. The seeds of fennel,

DILL

FENNEL

which is now also grown in America, are used in breads, cakes, and pastries, as well as in soups, sauces, and teas.

GARLIC

Garlic is a European herb, a member of the lily family, related to the onion and leek. The bulb is the part of the plant that is used. It is sometimes eaten as a vegetable in Europe, but its widest use is as a zesty seasoning for salads.

GINGER

Ginger, a plant native to India and China, has a pungent root stock that is used as a season-

GARLIC

GINGER

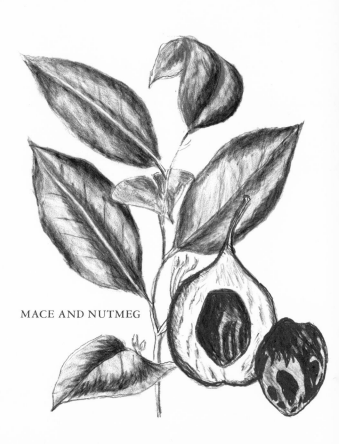

MACE AND NUTMEG

ing. Ginger was the first Oriental spice to be grown in the New World. In addition to being used as a seasoning, ginger is chewed to aid digestion or to soothe a toothache. It is a basic ingredient of at least six beverages, such as ginger ale and ginger beer.

MACE

The spice called mace is a part of the nutmeg that is prepared into a separate seasoning. Mace is a lacy, crimson-colored substance found in a thin layer under the husk of the nutmeg. It is carefully peeled away from the shell and spread out to dry before being further processed.

MARJORAM

Marjoram is one of the most popular herbs, a member of the mint family. It is a native of the Mediterranean region where it has been raised for centuries. The beautiful plant grows about a foot high, and has greenish gray leaves that are soft textured and covered with a delicate down. The plant makes a perfect seasoning for poultry stuffing and is used both in salads and as a garnish on them.

MUSTARD

Mustard has been used by man since prehistoric times. The leaves of the plant are eaten as salad greens and the seeds are ground to make seasoning. Prepared mustard has either turmeric or saffron added to it to produce the bright yellow color and sharp flavor we know.

NUTMEG

Nutmeg is one of the rarest and most famous spices. It was already well known by the Mid-

MARJORAM

MUSTARD

dle Ages. The best nutmegs grow in the West Indies where the trees reach a height of twenty-five feet. Yellow fruit the size of pears hang among the dark green, silver-lined leaves. The fruit is picked when it is ripe, and after the husk and the lining of mace have been removed, the nutmeg seed shell is left. When the seeds rattle it is a sign that the nutmeg has dried and can be removed from the shell.

OREGANO

Oregano, also a mint, is related to marjoram, but has a stronger flavor with a hot, biting undertone. The plant's deep green leaves dry

OREGANO

PAPRIKA

to a light green and are ground up for use in tomato and mushroom dishes, and with meat and chicken.

PAPRIKA

Paprika is prepared from the pods of certain cultivated sweet peppers. They were first found growing in Central America by the early Spanish explorers, but they are also native to India and New Guinea. Paprika is often used more for its bright red color than for its flavor.

PEPPER

Pepper has always been the most important of

all spices. In some places of the medieval world it was worth its weight in gold. Along with salt, pepper is our most familiar condiment.

Pepper is made from the dried berry of a woody, climbing East Indian vine. This pepper is no relation to the red and green sweet pod peppers or the hot red pod peppers. The pepper berries are picked before they ripen and are dried. They are then called peppercorns. The entire peppercorn, when ground, yields a powder of dark and light particles. White pepper is produced by separating the light core of the peppercorn from its dark skin.

Most of the world's pepper comes from the Malabar coast of India. Other pepper comes from Indonesia, Brazil, and Ceylon.

ROSEMARY

Rosemary, which originally grew on the rocky coasts of France and Spain, was known as rosmarinus, or sea dew. Its lacy foliage has a spicy sweet fragrance. An oil derived from the leaves

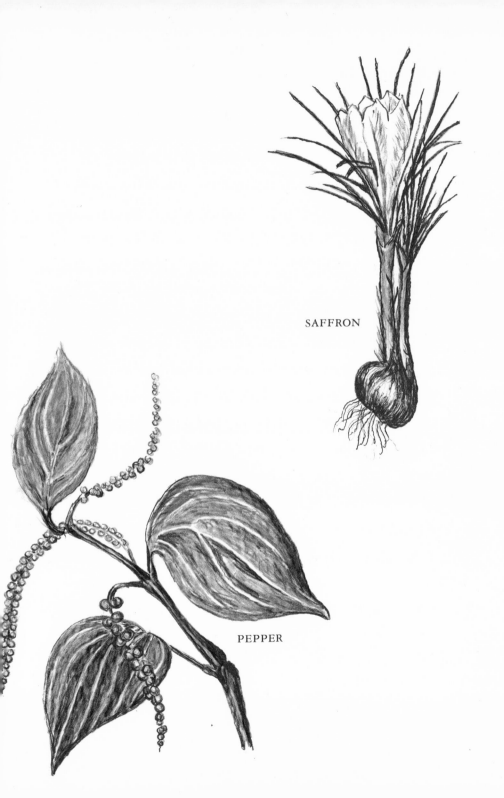

SAFFRON

PEPPER

is used in making cologne. Rosemary, either fresh or dried, is a seasoning for fruits, meats, and poultry. Traditionally, rosemary is the plant that denotes remembrance.

SAFFRON

Saffron is the most expensive spice, since the stigmas of 75,000 blossoms are needed to make one pound of saffron powder. The saffron crocus grows best in the meadows of Kashmir's Happy Valley, but it also is raised in Italy, France, and Spain. The Spanish are fond of its pungent flavor and its rich yellow coloring, and it usually appears in their favorite paella.

ROSEMARY

SAGE

Sage is the most widely used herb in the United States and probably in the world. It has been known universally as a good seasoning or flavoring since the earliest days of recorded history. A hardy perennial of about two feet in height, its leaves turn from sage green to gray and back to green at different seasons. The leaves are picked and dried for use in cooking.

SAVORY

Savory is an aromatic herb used all over southern Europe, because it brings out the flavor of many different foods, either singly or in combi-

SAGE

SAVORY

nation. There is both summer and winter savory; their flavors are similar, but the winter variety is slightly more pungent.

SESAME

Sesame is a native East Indian herb that has been used in the Far East for centuries. The small flat seeds of the plant are used for flavoring and an oil is also extracted from them. Sesame was introduced into this country by Negroes, who brought it from Africa. It now grows throughout this country and Canada.

TARRAGON

Tarragon is a hardy perennial thought to be

SESAME

native to southern Russia and western Siberia. The plant has been cultivated for five hundred years. The leaves have a pungent flavor and are widely used in cooking chicken, fish sauce, and in making tarragon vinegar.

THYME

Thyme is another herb of the large mint family. Its name, coming from the Greek word *thymon,* meaning sacrifice, was given to it because the herb was burned as incense in Greek temples. The fresh tops of thyme are served as a garnish; the leaves, either fresh or dried, are chopped to add flavor to a wide selection of cooked foods. All parts of the thyme plant are

TARRAGON

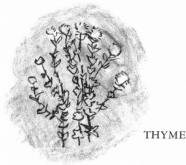

THYME

fragrant, and the volatile oil made from it is used in making perfume.

TURMERIC

Turmeric is one of the ancient spices of the ginger family, once used as a perfume as well as a spice. Native to China and Indonesia, it is now widely grown in India, Haiti, Jamaica, and Peru. As with ginger, the spice turmeric is taken from the roots of the plant, but its flavor is sweeter and more delicate than that of ginger. Turmeric is used in curry powder, and as a seasoning on its own.

TURMERIC

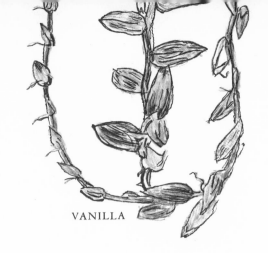

VANILLA

VANILLA

Vanilla is a flavoring extracted from the seed pods of an American climbing orchid plant. Cortes, the great Spanish explorer, was given a drink of chocolate flavored with vanilla beans by Montezuma, the Aztec emperor. Vanilla proved to be one of the most popular seasonings discovered by Cortes.

After harvesting, vanilla beans are carefully cured by warming them in the sun. They are then put in sweat boxes to ferment and produce the volatile oil with the delicious flavor. This oil, called vanillin, is then dissolved in alcohol and used in many food and ice-cream products and in perfumes.

INDEX

* Indicates illustration